POETRY RHYMES
For the Heart, Soul, and Mind

Linda Taylor

Poetry Rhymes for the Heart, Soul, and Mind
by Linda Taylor
Copyright ©2003, 2019 Linda Taylor

Photo Credit: Cover Photo by Malcolm Tyus Jr.

All rights reserved. No part of this book may be reproduced or transmitted in any form or by any means, electronic or mechanical, including photocopying, recording, or by any information storage and retrieval system without permission in writing from the copyright owner.

ISBN: 978-1-947829-93-0
For Worldwide Distribution
Printed in the U.S.A.

Please visit our website: diane-divine.com

Touch Point Productions & Publishing
Long Island, NY

*To my sisters and brothers
and significant others*

Contents

FAMILY *1*
Family *2*
My Daughter *3*
Baby Boy *4*
A Family *5*
Why Should I Change? *6*
Quality Time *7*
Another Place *8*
Mothers *9*
Fathers *10*
Grandma *11*
Grandpa *12*
Who I Am *13*

FAITH *15*
Faith *16*
Foolish People *17*
No Stress *18*
Keep On Smiling *19*
You Never Took Your Hands Off Me *20*
You Led Me *21*
The Blessing *22*
I Catch Myself *23*
Keep Your Mind on Jesus *24*
I Can't Complain *25*
Everything Is Working Out *26*
Just Another Blessing *27*
I Must Keep On Going *28*
Let me Live With You Above *29*
He Give Us *30*

Still Holding On   31
One Promise Will Remain   32
God's Gift to Me   33
I Have...   34
The Journey   35
Good Morning, Jesus   36
Battlefield of the Mind   37
New Challenges   38
Check it. Think it. Do it. Keep it.   39

LIFE   41
Life #1   42
Life #2   43
Ghetto   44
Flavor   45
We Don't Have To Agree   46
Special Time   47
Little Girl   48
We Live for the Moments   49
Don't Give Up   50
Make a Change   51
Sunday   52
Keeping It Real   53
Motivation   54
Difficult Situations   55
What's Most Important   56
Your Gift   57
Second Wind   58
Questions   59
Regroup   60
Get What You Need   61
Change the Pace   62
Material Things   63

Simple Poems   *64*
Teach   *65*
I'm Going To...   *66*
I Can Do It   *67*
Me   *68*
Bold Is the Word   *69*
I Write   *70*
Before and After   *71*
Stages   *72*
I Need More Space   *73*
What I Must Do   *74*
Shine   *75*
Many Phases   *76*
The Struggle   *77*
Someone Like You   *78*
Your Place   *79*

FRIENDS   *81*
Friends   *82*
Good Conversation   *83*
Special Friend   *84*
When Sisters Get Together   *85*
Positive Sisters   *86*
Celebrate Women   *87*
Help a Sister Out   *88*
For My Pleasure   *89*
Positive Brothers   *90*
Good Friends   *91*

Family

Family

Can't nobody do you like family!
That's what people say
For better or worse
They can be a blessing or curse
That's why it's so important to pray

They know you, and they don't
They'll help you, then they won't
Talk about you
Admire you
They want

They need
Take advantage
Do good and bad deeds
Yet and still, close
People you love the most

Always giving a helping hand
Even when you can't stand!
They are a part of your clan
Family is real
We all know the deal

My Daughter

It won't be long now
I claimed it a long time ago
I believe it is God's will
It will happen when God says so

A little life that lives in me
Will soon come out for the world to see

I await her arrival
With great joy in my heart
I love her so much already
I can't wait for her life to start

A little life that lives in me
Will soon come out for the world to see

Great learning experiences
I can't wait to share
With many hugs and kisses
And lots of love and care

A little life that lives in me
Will soon come out for the world to see

Baby Boy

I watch him breathe
I return his smile
I play with his fingers
I like his style

I rub his back
I play with his toes
I sing to him
I kiss his nose

My bundle of joy
My beautiful, bouncing, baby boy

A Family

I want us to be close
Like a family should be
Praying together
Sharing thoughts truthfully

Being able to talk about
Difficult times
Being good listeners
Easing each other's mind

Helping when we can
To make a situation right
Giving good advice
To fight the good fight

Showing love outward
Without hesitations
Being sincere
Without big presentations (drama)

Loving others
As we love ourself
Treating others respectfully
Taking good care of our health

Always knowing
That we are truly loved
Not just by our earthly family
But also by our Father above

Why Should I Change?

Why should I change
If it's really not me
Why should I do
If I'm not motivated to be
This different kind of person
That pleases someone else
Always making them happy
Forgetting about myself

Oh yes, I am important
My feelings matter too
But I guess I should try to compromise
And maybe do a little review
Of the way I am now
Maybe a little work I need
But we both must change some
If this relationship is going to succeed

Quality Time

No dress-up today
No spikes or high heels
I have on my jeans, tee shirt, and sneakers
I'm taking my son out for a happy meal

Maybe we'll go to a toy store
I'm sure he'd like that
I'm just hanging out with kids
Engaging in mother/son chitchat

My daughter's hanging out too
Oh I love it when she smiles and plays
We do our baby talk
Sometimes I think she understands what I say

Quality time is important
Togetherness makes children aware
That family is a strong, loving unit
Held together by parents and prayer

Another Place

Another place that I call home
Another place to be alone
Another place to gather my thoughts
Another place where I am boss

Another place to laugh and cry
Another place to quietly sigh
Another place where people may come
Another place to have some fun

Another place that's peaceful and calm
Another place where I am Mom
Another place my family loves
Our very own place
I thank God above

Mothers

You know
You do
You flow
You pursue

You console
You grow
You cajole
You glow

You stay
Make a way
Everyday
You pray

You pour out
your heart
Wise words
You impart

You are loved
Beyond compare
You are cherished
Here and there

You break
You recover
You ache
You discover

God gives you strength
God restores
And gives you so much more
You are a blessed mother
An awesome mother to the core

Fathers

For the ones who stayed around
Made an important impact
Not putting people down
For the ones who loved
From the heart
And tried to impart positivity

For the ones who always provided
Never hid
Always did
For the kids

For the ones who made you laugh
Dried your tears
Calmed your fears
Were sincere
And persevered
Hardworking
Soul searching
Faith imparting
Knowledge dropping
Life motivating
Communicating and creating
An environment of stability and love

For the ones who cared
And dared
And prepared
And were just there
We appreciate you
And love you
Right back

❧ Grandma ❧

Stepping in the family gap
Making provisions where there is lack
Sometimes loving from afar
Sometimes right up close and personal
Making better the scars

Grandmas can be:
Babysitters
Knowledge givers
Comforters
Problem solvers
Landlords
Lenders
Lovers
Givers

So many hats she wears
So many burdens she bears
Sharing
Caring
Staying
Praying

Whether near or far
Grandmas are shining stars

~ Grandpa ~

Always wanting to help
When he can
He'll sit you down
And share an important thought or plan

He'll tell you things
You may have never heard before
Share a new perspective
Which may open up a door

Supportive
Giving
Hardworking
Listening

Imparting wisdom and knowledge
Hoping one day you will acknowledge
They love to feel needed
A grandpa's love is undefeated

Who I Am

I am a mother
A daughter
An auntie
And a sister
A friend till the end
And a very good listener

I am a teacher
A writer
A playwright
And a poet
A quiet soul
With a heart of gold
A talented sister
Who can show it

I operate in these titles
But the one that is most special to me
I am a child of God
For He has defined me

Faith

Faith

Faith is believing
When all are against
An explanation for a miracle
That would otherwise not make sense

Even when signs of darkness
May slowly arise
Just not claiming the disappointment
But keeping your eye on the prize

Just knowing deep inside
That everything will work out
Don't give in to the fear
Don't turn away with doubts

Just let strength prevail
Thy will be done
When you were far from smiles
The victory was already won

Because of your faith

Foolish People

There are so many foolish people
Even I at times
Act as if I know not good sense
Confusion is all I find

And so it starts to consume me
Entering my every thought
But quickly I say
"Lord, take it away"

Please don't let me get caught
In a web of negative feelings
Causing me to act in negative ways
I know Your Spirit lives inside of me
This is where I want it to stay

So the foolishness starts to subside
I honestly wanted it to
It was giving me such headaches and heartaches
Thank You for bringing me through

No Stress

I don't know how it will turn out
But I don't stress
I just proceed in doing
My very best

Whatever the topic should be
I'll prepare my thoughts
I'll use the sense God gave me
And the things I've been taught

To move an audience
To touch a mind
To open a heart
Takes planning and time

So in doing all these things
There's no need to stress
I believe in myself
God has blessed

Keep On Smiling

I'm going to keep on smiling
Although negative vibes I feel
I'm going to keep on smiling
I know all wounds will heal

I know everyone won't like me
Or try to help at times
But I'm not ever worried
God's help I'll always find

I know God doesn't like ugly
So cordial I will be
I'm going to keep on smiling
God watches over me

You Never Took Your Hands Off Me

You never took Your hands off me
When You brought me into this world
You assured my mother
That she had a pearl

But it was inside this shell
It never opened wide
It was cared for and loved
It laughed and cried

You never took Your hands off me
When I pushed it open some
You let me experience things in this world
To see what I could become

Sometimes I fell down hard
Some things weren't meant to be
You let me find out the hard way
But that shell protected me

And then one day it opened
For all the world to see
I thank You each and every day
You never took Your hands off me

You Led Me

I know You led me
There could not have been any other way
I know it was You
All I did was pray

I know You led me
Where I needed to be
I know it was You
You always oversee

I know You led me
And let me proceed
I know it was You
Knowing exactly what I need

I know You led me
You knew this was the right choice
I know it was You
I heard Your voice

The Blessing

God works in mysterious ways
Greater misfortune could have happened
The situation could have been worse
But instead, You gave me a sign
A sign that I should take another look
Have things checked out again
Not settle for the way things are
Then came the blessing
Thanks, Lord, for looking out

I Catch Myself

I catch myself so often
In my thoughts, words, and deeds
Thinking, saying, doing
Things that I have no need

Asking for forgiveness
Wondering what He says
When people let ignorance get the best of them
And act without using their heads

He is all forgiving
But what about those who don't ask
Or care about the consequences
When common sense and faith lack

I guess I can just pray for the people
And hope that by some miraculous way
Their lives will eventually turn around
And they will want to live for You each day

Keep Your Mind on Jesus

Keep your mind on Jesus
Let your thoughts be as His
At least as much as possible
So better lives you can live

Without worrying so
About problems and cares
You must bring them to the Lord
And leave them there

If your so-called good intentions hurt
Or try to pull one down
Consider this question
What would the Lord do if He were around

Would His actions be different
His thoughts, more wise
I believe so

I Can't Complain

I don't feel great all the time
But I can't complain
God has allowed me to live happily
With minimal pain
And great gains
Bringing me safely through the rain

Yes, I did get wet
And I'll never forget
The lessons that He has taught me
You see it was a part of the plan
That one day I'd eventually take my stand

And truly learn who I am
And my purpose
Is to help and love
Constantly thanking God above
Oh no, I can't complain

Everything Is Working Out

Everything is working out
Just like I believed it would
I'll always believe in my heart
Things work together for good

To those that love the Lord
And are called to do His will
The Lord will work everything out
If I'd just remain still

And not take any drastic actions upon myself
That are not spiritually motivated to do
Not giving me any praise
But being focused all on You

Just Another Blessing

Just another blessing
You've given to me
I thank You, Lord
So adamantly

I claimed it
Just like You said I should do
And then it happened
Your promise came through

As it always does
At just the right time
Not a minute too late
Now everything is fine

I Must Keep On Going

I must keep on going
This isn't the end
I do have a little
But there's so much within

How will I discover
What I have yet to know
If I'm settled with now
And the little I show

I must always continue
My work is not done
My race is not over
My victory not all won

It is those who endure
Through the pain that we face
Who'll be a recipient of His promise
And dwell in His place

The never-ending journey
With experiences untold
A door that will never close
For the key He holds

A goal that continues forever
And you will sow just what you reap
A stand you'll always take
A promise you'll always keep

I must keep on going
The sureness is there
But I know there is so much more
I will have to bear

My life is not over
Not all is fulfilled
And I will not stop
Until it is God's will

Let Me Live With You Above

Stand by me when I am weak
Help me find what I must seek
Stand by me when I must lead
Help me care for other's needs

Help me learn what You think I should know
Lead me in the direction You think I should go
Stand by me when I don't understand
Let my mind say, "Yes I can"

Let me live a life with love
Then let me live with You above

He Gives Us

He gives us the stars
He gives us the moon
He gives us the mornings
The nights and the noon

He gives us the time
He gives us the will
If we want to accomplish
He gives us the skill

He gives us pain
He gives us sorrow
He gives us the days
With hope for tomorrow

He gives us our mind
And to each his own
He gives us some moments
To be all alone

He gives us beauty
Inside and out
He gives us awareness
He gives us doubts

God gives His children
So many things
He gives us special love
That only He can bring

He gives us a chance
To show real love
He gives us a chance
To live up above

Still Holding On

I'm still holding on
To Your everlasting grace
I'm still holding on
Through the trials I face

I'm still holding on
Though the road may get hard
I'm still holding on
Because I feel no ways tired

If I would have believed
All these different things people are saying
Instead of in myself
And the power in praying

Then I would have let go
Such a long time ago
But the truth is I know
I am aware
Of the power in prayer

One Promise Will Remain

Look at the flowers
Don't you know one day they're going to die
Just like we can't live forever
Or shine every day in our lives
Now those flowers
Don't you know they have felt the rain
But after the storm was over
They have grown

When you apply that to your life right away
Then you may come to know
That in this world we will all
Have our ups and downs
But all through the pain
And through the rain

And even in the midst of the storm
He has made a way for us
And we will learn
There are a lot of things we don't know
But one day God to us will show

As He has made it this way
One day we will see
That all the things in this world
Will one day no longer be
Except His promise He made to us
To set us free

God's Gift to Me

I would like to apply
the answer to my why
To what I asked it for
So that I might learn more

If I could just perceive
The knowledge that I'm learning
And honestly conceive
I'd satisfy my yearning

At least I am aware
But really not all there
The answer is in my mind
But quickly I can't find

Help me to know
What I don't understand
And apply it to my reason
I don't mind reprimand

Because through it, I will learn
And then I'll truly know
God's grace has brought me through
This gift I have to show

The triumph's not in me
My faith has got me by
No other will I owe
No other do I know

That's why I do believe
And follow in His path
This world can't give me anything
That my God doesn't have

I do not need to please the world
Just show what God gave to me
And let His will be done
To live eternally

I Have...

I have rhythm and rhyme
Vision for this time
Persistence and the will
Wisdom to do or keep still

I have faith when I don't see
Knowing God gave me the victory
I have discernment and joy
God's protection so the enemy can't destroy

I have humility and calm
Knowledge from the Psalms
I have this life that God gave me
To make a difference and be free

The Journey

Thank You for the journey
I walk through everyday
Thank You for the fresh ideas
And the creative energy You give me to display

Thank You for the appointed time
And this appointed place
Thank You for the obstacles
I thought I couldn't face

Thank You for the strength You gave
When peace was hard to find
Thank You for sending me help
Right in the nick of time

Thank You for my quiet times
Even in the midst of noise
Thank You for Your calmness
And the simple little joys

Thank You for Your mercy
As my worldly side shows face
Thank You for forgiveness
And covering me with Your grace

Thank You for the plans
You have predestined just for me
They give me hope and a future
That's very bright to see

Good Morning, Jesus

Good morning, Jesus
You're such a glorious sight
Good morning, Jesus
Stayed with me all through the night
I prayed and prayed
For You to turn things around
Now I no longer wear a frown

Good morning, Jesus
In my life, You're here to stay
I'm glad I met You
And You saved my soul one day
I start each day out
Just by saying to You
Thank You, Jesus, I love You

I'm praising You now
Can't stop it, no how
Please don't ever leave me alone
I've got my Sunday praise
Going straight through Monday praise

Good morning, Jesus
You're such a glorious sight
Good morning, Jesus
I'm feeling better day and night
Now our relationship is solid and true
Good morning, Jesus
I love You

Battlefield of the Mind

Battlefield of the mind
Satan is trying to get mine
He wants to control my thoughts
So peace I can't find

There's an open invitation
The party is on
Do you stay and engage
No, try and stay strong

The best weapons we have are prayer and praise
I will use them during the struggle
I know I'll be amazed
At what God can do

He was waiting all the time
For me to get my act together
So now I see the signs
I will guard my heart and mind

Using constant prayer and praise
As I worship God
I'll come out with my hands raised

In victory
In thankful adoration
I'm so glad God doesn't go on vacation

New Challenges

Every day is a new challenge
Lord, You know my heart
I believe in my spirit
You set me apart

To do a great work
To which You will show
You'll guide me with Your grace
To where I need to go

Sometimes extreme sadness
Overtakes my mind
I become preoccupied with thoughts
Of leaving folks behind

But I believe there is a greater good
to which I need to strive
When I engage in worship and praise
My feelings start to subside

I feel my strength kick in
And assurance in my soul
Although I'll experience uncertainty
I will achieve my goal

For I know the plans and thoughts I have for you," says the Lord. "Plans for peace and well-being and not for disaster, to give you a future and a hope (Jeremiah 29:11 AMP).

Check it. Think it. Do it. Keep it.

Check it:
Check yourself and your attitude
Pray about it, even if you're not in the mood
Check your thoughts, check your words, check your deeds
Check your personality—we all have needs

Think it:
Righteous thoughts and on God's goodness
Positive thoughts will help you get through the mess
Think about how Jesus died for your sins
Giving us a chance to live with Him in the end

Do it:
All you can to help out
Friends and acquaintances who have troubles and doubts
Do the right things, letting others see Christ in you
You may be the only Jesus they have to look to

Keep it:
God's words in you
Keep His light shining so others can see through
Keep a praise in your mouth
Keep joy in your heart
That's what life is all about

Check it
Think it
Do it
Keep it

LIFE

Life #1

Life is what you make it
Life is what you do
Life is the frazzle and dazzle
Of everything that composes you

And where you are
And just how far
It will take you
To reach your shining star

Your special thing
That makes you sing
It's the process
That takes you out of your mess

The life test
To find success
Like all the rest
And truly be blessed

Life #2

Life is daily living and giving
With lots of storylines
Life is what God has given
Life is not always defined

Life is more that your existence
It's what you set out to do
It's an awesome place or an empty space
You'll have to choose from the two

Life can be so hectic with so much to do
Or life can be so plain and so mundane
With no focus, no vision, no clue
Always make the best out of life

Smile and help others when you can
Life is very precious
Work out your purpose and plan
You are only given a certain lifespan

Ghetto

Ghetto
Really what does it mean
Is it a place
With a negative theme

Is it a person
Less sophisticated than another
Less skilled in life
Than other sisters and brothers

Is it a way of life
When a dream is deferred
When a life is shattered
When the world seems obscured

Is it a race of people
In a horrible place
With no way out
With a history they can't erase

Is it a reality
With bitter laughter and smiles
With hope, joy, and faith
Being applied every once in awhile

It's maybe all of this
Or none of this at all
Ghetto is powerful history
It's also a wake-up call

Flavor

When you add flavor
To ordinary talk
You get more personality and attitude
You get a spicy sauce

You get a deep, rich feeling
That could only come from the soul
You get smoked ham hocks in collard greens
And butter on a toasted roll

When you add flavor
To a party or affair
Things just aren't ordinary
There's drama and extra flair
You may even see my new hair (style)

We Don't Have To Agree

You have your thoughts
Well I have mine too
A difference of opinion
To thine own self be true

We don't have to agree
On every little thing
I may like to dance
You may like to sing

I might think it's wrong
The reason I give may not be acceptable to you
We may be at it all night long

I hear your opinions loud and clear
I respect your thoughts and style
We don't have to agree
We just have to end with a smile

Special Time

Ten o'clock at night
This is my special time
The kids are asleep
I can finally unwind

I sit in my big, comfy chair
I close my eyes and rest
I've been constantly going all day
Now there is no stress

I'm in a relaxed state of mind
But I want to do some positive things too
So I take out my journal and write
Putting down my points of view

Then I slowly doze off to sleep
Thanking God for another day
This special time I had
Really turned out okay

Little Girl

Little girl
Want to grow up so fast
Little girl
The feeling will soon pass
Don't try to rush the things
That will naturally come

Little girl
You're still a child
All those things will take a while
So don't give up and say they won't happen

We should never forget
And keep in mind
All things will happen
When God says it's time

So be patient
He won't forget you
All we have to do is keep believing

We Live for the Moments

We live for the moments
We cherish the years
When not victory's glory
We will shed the tears

We live for the times
We preciously share
When all is not rosy
There's pain we must bear

We live for the moments
When love is at bloom
And then the separations
That happen too soon

We live for the time
When we will succeed
We live for the moments
When we'll have the lead

We wish for the day
When all wars will cease
And that glorious moment
When we'll live in peace

Don't Give Up

Whatever you do, don't say you can't
If you truly believe, you can
If not alone or by yourself
Someone else will give you a hand

Don't give up the race before it's through
Finish it to the end
If you want to be victorious
You must earnestly strive to win

If at first you do not succeed
At least you did your best
If you are to be successful in this field
You will eventually pass the text

When you're discouraged, feeling low
And filled with misery
You just have to remember
For awhile, this is meant to be

The world is so imperfect
There is so much going wrong
If you want to achieve anything in life
You must work hard and long

You must remember Your Creator
The One who helps you through
Your daily tribulations
He makes them all so few

You must never give up hope
You must always believe
He gave us a chance in life
To fail and to achieve

Whichever we decide to do
I guess is up to us
All I can say is, never give up
This, I feel, is a MUST

∽ Make a Change ∽

You can't think about
What could have been
Time has passed
You must go on

Dwelling on the past
Could be detrimental to you
Let it go
You must go on

Things could have been different if.....
You constantly say
If I only had...
Won't make it go away
You must go on

Concentrate on correction
And making things better
It's not the end of the world
You can make a change

Sunday

Sunday morning
We got to sleep a little late
My Momma used to wake us up
With a good breakfast at half past eight

Sometimes it was eggs and sausage
Accompanied with biscuits and grits
Some days she'd make salmon croquettes
Or pancakes and omelets

We'd go to Sunday School
To learn about God and pray
I can't tell you I remembered so much
But I learned how to respect and obey

My Momma always came to church
After Sunday School was through
She wouldn't let us sit just anywhere
But that's an issue we later outgrew

After church was over
We'd go home and put our play clothes on
Momma would finish cooking dinner
Singing some of her gospel songs

And that's the way our Sunday went
It really was a special time
We all sat at the dinner table together
In a peaceful state of mind

Most of the time

Keeping It Real

Keeping it real
What else could I do
Try to be fake and phony
And fool one or two

Deny what I am
To be what they are
Walking around funny
Trying to be a movie star

Looking past the pain
Trying to be abstract
Over the smallest problems
I overreact

Drawing unnecessary attention
For my own special gain
Finding pleasure
In another person's pain

No, I'm keeping it real
Drama is good sometimes
But if it just isn't you
Then heed the warning sign

Be true to yourself
And the others you meet
No need to put on airs
Just be upbeat
Or discreet
But don't be a deadbeat

Motivation

Let motivation move you
You may have to do it right now
If it is an appropriate time
You should make a way somehow

Make every minute matter
Nonsense is so easy to do
Some people engage in foolishness so readily
Time is wasted through and through

Groom yourself to be ready
So when it's really your time
You will glisten
And they'll always listen
Then you will truly shine

Difficult Situations

Difficult situations may arise
As they so often do
When you're trying to accomplish something
Or see a situation through

More and more confusion becomes added
Just when you think you've solved it all
The situation expands for the worse
Putting back against the wall

But this is nothing new
It happens all the time
And how we handle it
Sometimes gets out of line

Keep the faith and persevere
Don't listen to negative thoughts in your ear
If you fall, you'll be okay
Just try again a different way

If all else fails, just take it in stride
Chalk it up as a learning experience
In the future, you'll be more wise

What's Most Important

What's most important
Some might ask
The present and now
Or the future or past
They all are
But the now is the most important of all
The past,
We should learn from
Fondly remember
Or try to forget
The future we don't even know
But the present
How we are
How we give
How we live
Is the most important of all

Your Gift

When God gives you a gift
It's not a tale or myth
You really need to use it
And definitely not abuse it

Use it to give the Lord praise
And more awareness raise
Of His power, mercy, and grace
Love the Lord and He'll steady your pace

～ Second Wind ～

I can't think when I'm tired
But it's hard to get to sleep
I put the TV on low
Then I try to get deep

In my thoughts and my dreams
I meditate for awhile
A notion pops in my mind
that really gets me riled

I can't shake it off
It's got me in a tailspin
I better put on some tea
Here comes my second wind

❧ Questions ❧

Am I scared?
A little.
Will I be okay?
I guess.
Will I lose it?
I hope not.
Will I be strong?
I'll try.
Will others encourage me?
Not always.
Will it really matter?
Somewhat.
Can I really do it?
I believe so.
Will I stop trying if I fail?
Not for long.

～ Regroup ～

Sometimes you have to back away
Then turn around and pursue again
Use a different approach
A different strategy to win

Always sticking to your guns
Just putting them back in holsters at times
Always believing deep in your heart
The power in all the signs

Why did the idea surface
Why was the fire lit again
Why is determination growing in me
I'm more sure than I've ever been

You'll find that whatever you're hoping
Will slowly unveil itself or change
Or come to full circle
Or be in agreement
Or completely rearrange
Or happen just the way you like

Get What You Need

Realization
You already knew
There were extra things
You needed to do
But you didn't know how
Now it's up to you

Go get what you need
To find what you seek
In order to truly succeed
You'll need some new techniques
You can't come out weak
So take heed
Get what you need

Change the Pace

I know I don't do enough
Laziness overcomes my mind
And of course my body follows
It happens all the time

How do you prevent this from happening
How do you change the pace
And become more active and bubbly too
Your life no longer a waste

I have some things going on
For short times here and there
But I need to feel a constant urge
So I can stay aware

Of the busy intriguing world around us
That welcomes me each day
And feel in my heart
To stay a part
And not let life slip away

Material Things

Oh that's nice
It looks good over there
We need one more piece
To make this room complete
I want this one in brown
Or maybe in mahogany
These stools will look good at the counter
We need a shaggy rug
To lay under the china cabinet
We need another television for upstairs
Satisfaction for the moment
Won't last for a lifetime
Material things help you decorate
And accentuate
And in some ways sophisticate
You may even appreciate
But all these things
Don't really mean a thing
You need something stronger
To help you go longer
To stay kind
In the right frame of mind
Just remember that
As you start your collection

Simple Poems

I write simple poems
Just because I can
I write simple poems
So people will understand

I write simple poems
So knowledge, others will reap
I write simple poems
The messages are easy to keep

I write simple poems
To brighten up my day
I write simple poems
To show others the way

I write simple poems
Intense they still might be
I write simple poems
They are just a part of me

Teach

This is what I have to do
To let my light shine through and through
For this, I was professionally schooled
And blessed by God to use these tools
He gave to me, not to keep inside
But to share with others
So they may abide
To touch a child
To fill a heart
To change a mind
What a good start

I'm Going To...

I'm going to set the tone
Show you how things should be
If you're having trouble following along
Then you need to ask somebody

I'm going to lay the groundwork
Establish a good rapport
Make sure things are ready
Back it up with good support

It's going to turn out right
Planning has taken place
Things are as they should be
Encompassed with grace

I Can Do It

You know I can hook it up
Then it will be fly
You know it will be slammin'
I always satisfy

I can fix it up right
And put the cherry on top
Add some chocolate syrup
The cream of the crop

I can do it up good
Don't you worry about a thing
You know I always come through
I'll take care of everything

I can set it off
Without a doubt
Do what I need to do
And stay strong throughout

 Me

I can play the part
And be all smiles
Mesmerize you
With my feminine wiles

Be dynamic
And outspoken too
Speak to my people
And always be true

I can also be quiet
Unassuming at most
Just watching others
As they tell stories or boast

There are two sides of me
You don't always see
I present them when needed
In different degrees

I have the controls
I click off or on
This is how I am
It's a phenomenon

Bold Is the Word

"Bold" is the word
Haven't you heard
I'm going to do my thing
Fly free as a bird

Cherish each day
As if it were the last
And in His love
I'll stay steadfast

Make a difference
In my own kind of way
Not putting off for tomorrow
What I can do today

Standing strong
For what I believe
Staying calm through the nonsense
So I won't be deceived

So bold is the word
Positive actions should impact
Feel good about yourself and what you do
Don't worry about what you lack

Just use whatever you have
To get your point heard
To make your stand
And be in command
Remember bold is the word

I Write

Whenever I get inspiration
A premonition
Or feeling frustration
Or uncertain feelings
I just can't explain
Or I'm so elated
Lifted to a higher plain

Whenever I'm lonely
Not much to do
With too many bills to pay
Waiting on my breakthrough
Whenever I'm touched by emotions
Overcome by desires
Feeling the spirit
From the sounds of a choir
I write

Before and After

When I was a kid
My life was so free
I played silly games
Pretending to be

Each day was fulfilling
I learned and had fun
Then everything would start over
When yesterday was done

My life was so simple
My dreams were so real
Most of them came true
They weren't big deals

Now I no longer pretend
Life isn't the same
More responsibility
More chances for gain

Now in my mind
I'll always conceive
My new dreams will happen
I'll always believe

It may take some time
For we must realize
We don't always get those things
We fantasize

They'll be more realistic
My ambitions and goals
Although I don't really know
What the future holds

Stages

Inconspicuously I walk
Not wanted them to know
He sees my faults

Confidently I try
Not really knowing how
He shows me

Respectably I do
I want them to know
He knows my time

Fearfully I shake
I get nervous
He comforts me

Embarrassing I turn
They laugh
I'll still make it

Quietly I cry
Through my trials
He dries my tears

Knowledgeably I know
Right from wrong
He has taught me

Faithfully I believe
I'll always know He loves me

Patiently I wait
Never by myself
I won't give us

I Need More Space

I need more space
To stretch out
To do
To put
To take
To experiment
To venture
To sing
To act
To dance
To rest
To be
Myself

What I Must Do

I want to do something
Positive with my life
I want to be a leader
But first I must listen
I must learn
I must get
I must earn
I must know
All the knowledge I can
I must grow
To be better than I am

Shine

I'm going to shine
Like the noonday sun
I'm going to work
Till this day is done

And then start again
Till the next day's end
And cover more ground
Till this battle I win

And how might that happen
You'll never believe
But I do have the confidence
It takes to achieve

And you too can have
What it takes to be strong
To go through this world
Changing wrong

Making it right
Stopping the fights
Reasoning together
To gain new heights

Loving and growing
Still taking the lead
Remembering where you came from
And always taking heed

Many Phases

Many phases
Many stages
Many parts
On many pages

Turn each one slowly
Read each word
The underlying mysteries
May be inferred

If you can't decipher
Don't assume the worse
Maybe you're not
Completely immersed

Read it again
With proper discernment
Then maybe you'll see
The intended sentiment

The Struggle

We, as a people, have struggled so much
Suffered as such—felt as if all hope was gone
But between you and me, it has made me strong
Although our treatment was wrong
No one cared about that

This is why we have to stand the test
Being our very best
Not letting anything hold us back
Being bold and black
Doesn't always bring contentment,
When construed as militant
They don't understand, that's just how I am
Intellectually we have to let them see

There's more to you and me than they will ever know
Maybe not status quo, but just letting our talents flow
Through it all we will grow and continue to show
That we are a force and a powerful source
So let's stay on course and always reinforce

Our goals, our plans
And continue to expand
Our outlook and capabilities
And in some respect, stay on our knees
Praying and having faith

That all things will be what they will be
We're slated to have despair and tranquility
But through it all
We will
Remain free

Someone Like You

Someone like you has come before,
Standing up for our people, opening a door.
Someone like you has already won the race,
Doing all they could to stay with the pace.
Someone like you has already taken the lead,
Domineering, persevering, planting a seed.
And when the plant grew, then here comes you!
Spreading your branches, taking bold chances.
Not afraid of the fire,
Knowing more wood will make the flames grow brighter.
But don't get caught up and start to desire the forbidden fruits,
Or you'll fall into that same conflict as Adam and Eve
And you'll have to leave your place in the spotlight,
And lay low, out of sight until you get your act right.
So you fight the good fight. We won't always be correct,
So don't expect that everything will be perfect.
Things will eventually turn out okay,
But there's always going to be conflict along the way.
Just stay strong and pray!
If things were meant to be, then your story will end successfully
Or with bittersweet memories of a tragic end but then again...
The legacy will still live on.
All the positive things you did will be remembered in song.
And...with programs that aren't too long.
But most of all, we'll remember in our hearts and minds,
And think of you fondly from time to time
As we sit back and unwind, applying your struggle to our time.
And in some ways, we're still in total accord,
Struggling for our rewards, still moving slowly toward our place,
Changing pace to fit our present situation.
The past has given a foundation so we can reach our destination
Because of someone like you who already made it through.

Your Place

We used to have to know our place
In a world where white power reared its ugly face.
We used to step lightly, always watching our backs,
Owned as property and freedom we lacked.
But we overcame and things aren't exactly the same
As they were years before.

Some of our people are still imprisoned by lack of knowledge
Has nothing to do with going to college.
Just afraid to expand, fearing some woman or man,
Or some negative situation or just shear procrastination.
Let me share with you my recommendation:

Read a powerful book and get hooked,
Listen to someone you admire or someone who inspires,
See what they're talking about.
It may take away some of your fears and doubts,
And give you some new ideas as to how to proceed.

Make a list of the things you need to do to pursue your goal.
Now you may have to stand strong and be bold.
You may even come across as being cold.
But we can't be bubbly and loving all the time.
Sometimes your attitude needs to be:

"I'm going to get mine" for we can't always act so refined.
But do watch out for the warning signs.
Let's be correct in our dealings, not hurting everyone's feelings.
Intelligence has to come acrosss.
Sometimes you just may be the co-worker, not the boss

So take all your successes in stride.
God will always provide exactly what you need.
Disappointments help you to grow

And ignite regrouping when you're dealt a hard blow,
Helping you get back on track with a new attitude
Or point of view or more courage you lacked before.
Now you can open that door
And know your place in a positive way
Don't forget to pray.
God will always make a better day.

FRIENDS

Friends

We didn't have to search for
Particular words to say
We weren't trying to impress
With language
Other than everyday

We talk about different people
Our children
Our husbands
Our friends
We talk on different topics
From beginning to end

At least an end for now
We'll talk again real soon
It's such a positive feeling
Knowing we're all fine-tuned

Good Conversation

Good conversation
Stimulates the mind
And is good for the soul
I love to have it all the time

With family and friends
It's really great
We'll just talk and talk for hours
Almost forgetting it's getting late

We have to go to work tomorrow
Kids have to go to school
But this time was so refreshing
It gave me a lot of fuel

Special Friend

You've been so helpful
Through it all
I know on you
I could always call

You cleaned and brought
Gave advice and taught
And through it all
We never verbally fought

This is a good sign
You were so kind
Maybe one day
We'll celebrate over wine
Good people like you
Are hard to find

When Sisters Get Together

When sisters get together
Honey child, honey child, honey child
When sisters get together
You know it's going to get loud

We'll sit and talk for hours
Sharing stories left and right
Getting the 411 gossip just for fun
Sometimes we'll hang out all night

When sisters get together
Oh yes, we're on our game
When sisters get together
We may talk about old and new flames

When sisters get together
What drama, pizzazz, and appeal
When sisters get together
You know the deal

Positive Sisters

Positive sisters
Doing important things in this world
Showing out
Without a doubt
We are chocolate cover girls

Positive sisters
Making a way with what we have
Building up others
Encouraging our sisters and brothers
Leading children down a correct path

Positive sisters
Have you ever wondered
How we got this way
We overcame the struggles
And prayed to God for better days

Oh yes, He answered our prayers
That's what makes positive sisters so strong
When all is a mess
That's when we're at our best
We do what we have to do
Then positive sisters sing their song

Celebrate Women

Celebrate women
All over the world
We are the mothers
Who bore little boys and girls

Who reared them in right directions
In fortunate occasions, a positive male did assist
But sometimes we had to do it all alone
Praying constantly
So ills, we could resist

Sometimes we had to be creative
Doing something with little or nothing at all
We always knew we had to make out own way
Being strong
Being bold
Standing tall

Celebrate women
With a history of steadfast love and durable faith
Who are truly great inspirations
We should always embrace

Help a Sister Out

Help a sister out sometimes
Say an encouraging word or two
Help celebrate with us
The positive things we do

Try to understand a sister
And the mentality behind
The little things she does
That aren't always defined

Comfort a sister when needed
You might not always see the outward signs
Which makes it a little difficult to do
You see, we don't always sit around and whine

We're only distraught for a moment
Strength enters our body and mind
We fixed that little problem
Now everything is just fine

Now don't rub a sister the wrong way
Oh you don't want to ever do that
You may see so much emotion, attitude, and drama
You just pushed up her thermostat

For My Pleasure

Not for gain
Not for show
Not for parties
With people we know

Not for position
Not for power
Not to brag about
Every hour

Not to keep up with the Joneses
The Thomases or the Smiths
Just for my own pleasure
So I can share with

Positive people
And have a spiritually fulfilling time
On my own turf
Good food for the mind

Positive Brothers

Positive brothers, taking on life,
Supporting a sister or maybe a wife.
Making decision that affect the whole,
Producing good situations, prosperity unfolds.
Not thinking he knows it all,
Consulting others when he needs,
A strong family type, looking good in dungarees.
Taking care of his business, coming to you correct
Having faith in God, showing respect.
Responding to your needs, whether big or small,
Down with the struggle of justice for all.
Taking an interest in the little things you do,
Uplifting, supporting, and encouraging you.
Comforting others when they need a friend,
A strong shoulder to cry on, on him you can depend
Positive brothers, why can't they all be that way?
I'm sad to say that some have gone astray.
We have to claim them back. Build them up where they lack.
Give them the skills to pay the bills,
Lead them back on the right track.
As a matter of fact…we can do this in several ways.
Let's dispel the myths they want black males to portray.
What you visually see, may not always be,
Let's not prejudge our black males to a certain degree.
Give them love and understanding, not always reprimanding,
Create a web of trust.
Establish a climate that all parties have discussed.
Positive brothers are and always will be
The strongest and boldest commodity,
Out of he came the she,
So we will stand by your side and not let our efforts subside.
God will guide.

~ Good Friends ~

Are:
Caring and kind
Good company for cheese and wine
Honest and real
Possessing unique appeal

Supportive and concerned
They live what they've learned
Wise
In many ways
I love them
Always

About the Author

Linda Taylor has molded kids' lives as a teacher for more than 25 years. She uses her poetry, songs, and chants in her kindergarten classroom to enhance learning and motivate her students. Linda holds an M.S. degree in Education from C.U.N.Y. at City College. She's the author of the Amazing Annabelle series, which has eleven chapter books and the Daring David series, which also has eleven chapter books. Linda lives with her family in Long Island.

She has also authored three other poetry books:
ALPHABET, NUMBER, AND COLOR POETRY
POEMS THROUGHOUT THE YEAR AND BEYOND
REALLY COOL ANIMAL POEMS